When the Light is Mine

poetry for the people

CHAZ HOLESWORTH

Contents

Introduction

My name is Chaz Holesworth, and this is my first poetry collection. It is strung together to show everyone how the world has made me feel throughout the decades.

These poems were written during my darkest, most mentally draining moments, as I searched for the meaning of life, love, and whatever God is. They focus on my experiences and perspectives, while trying to make sense of things.

I don't know how to describe my style, but some say I write stream-of-consciousness poetry with a lyrical quality. That makes sense since the lyrics to my favorite songs are my biggest inspiration. Most of my writing occurs when I have an urge to express myself. Sometimes, I have an idea, and other times I type on my laptop and see where it takes me.

The themes of this collection come from my struggles with poverty, a dysfunctional family, an extreme Christian fundamentalist upbringing, society's faults, my distaste for the government, and love (or the lack of it). With it comes the pain and borderline insane thoughts that rushed through my mind while typing away. I hope one can find meaning or comfort in knowing they are not alone with these thoughts, whether it be about organized religion or having OCD and severe self-loathing - two things that come up often in my writing.

Thank you for listening to the holler.

Everything in its Right Place

Condescending Towards the Midas Touch

Self-deprecating to beat them to the punch,
their lack of empathy has endangered trust.
Human rights have become polarized,
while the right human traits have taken refuge.

The cashiers can't keep up with the cons,
bits to bits, and cryptic invisible relics.
Sell a mindset, sell the future, sell the future, their version of culture.

Golden flying palaces to keep one intrigued,
stolen land murmurs of ongoing grief.
Sleight of hand has never been so transparent, but knees aren't meant
to bend this much.

The Minus touch is rampant as clingy kings pull the strings.
Winners of constant losing wars,
counting their coins in the clouds,
as the have-nots keep bending the knee.

Thinking of the Times When I Went Wrong

The nature of things to come - tell me more about your prize in times.
The lecture says we need to recline, the sector says we need to refine.
The elastic pulls on my nylon heart; I listen to the nonsense loud.

Cradled in fear like it is the blanket of doubt, I came around and saw
the telling tale of my selling out.
I ran for the bunkers and wished for my atoms to dissolve.

Kept my feet on the fire and listened to the holler for help.
These things that take shape will always be familiar; the backdrop will
always whistle my failures.
I crave redemption like it was sold by Pharma crooks. I laugh at my
follies to pretend I am in on the joke.

Memories are just samples of when things made sense.
The structure of sound and sight keeps us grounded.
The listener ignores the parts that do not fit their ego.
I was alone when I saw who was to blame.

The Ghost of My Personality in a Cookie-Cutter Shape

I'm Antichrist as long as they're not antitrust,
fire under one's feet, sort of moral traits.

Selling drivel with cleavage shots
and baby-like skin, with jingles that are a waste of musical notes.

Feed the poor and cold, starve the feverish rich.

The storm is coming, says the quack, looking for views.

Can everyone's fifteen minutes be over now?
I knew we lost when humans became brands.

Give the clown the crown and see how much more we're endangered.

Shooting fast talkers in slow motion to slow down the spin.
Catch and bury on every résumé, as long as the dark money keeps
pouring in, the citizens will only be united in suffering.

Lack of interest and live-in-the-moment routines have them pulling
fast ones with their reality smoke machines.

Give me a holler and sell me a dollar,
the future was never meant for the long haul -just enough time to let
the bastards eat caviar while we suck on the crumbs of their fables.

Just Trying to be a Good Contestant in the System That's Geared to the Highest Bidder

The language I kept was only prominent in my mind,
the stage we set is to make them rich enough to hide.

The gains I made only cost me my soul,
like dreamers whose nightmares become lucid,
like those who think failure is the inevitable norm,
and when the land of the free is only for those who can afford it.

"Give me a break," said the last guard on duty,
who was sent to protect us from fatigue.
Candle makers in the era of electricity.
Shortage of thinkers for the instant gratification clause. I kindle the
idea that I'm only as old as my cells.

Victory in salvage trails, coughing cups and resounding air,
the land is used for the taming.
Candy locks and bubble gum trials, salty breath and seaweed diets,
fabric clothes for dusty noobs, tragic tales of lingering doom.
Give me your thoughts, and I will fall asleep often.
Tortured words that rhyme, the kids have lazy poetry eyes.

Thinking is torture, feeling is obsolete.
I've met my falter, and it's stuck on repeat.

I Wear My Grin Like an Insecurity Blanket

Too much has happened. Now sadness is a luxury.
The demons are ahead. The demons have filled in the holes.

I cast away my lonely parts for any chance of feeling whole.
Burning stars are a wake-up call to know when it's time to leave.

Caving in and selling trends is what it takes to stay even.
The cast of dust is lining up to be the next final showing.
I'm holding on to future tones that will keep the path going.
The longing for a clearer tone will never be a pardon for the lecture of
their torment.
I gave too much to care too much.

And silence now is my peer.
The point is less; the meaning isn't full.
I can't recall my self-worth.

So, I'm off to neglect my feelings some more.
You hold us hostage with our fears of death, making a killing on the
unknown. Make us slaves to rituals and folklore, as long as our credit
scores are intact.

Introvert/extrovert

Introvert or extrovert, take your pick.

Depends on which wounds to lick.
Catch a cold from demon toads, and the wrath is just desserts.

The will of the problem is greater than the solutions,
which is why we'll never get it right.
The slavers have a new waiver they impose, telling us to consume the
status quo like it's our only option. Can't be left out.

Fever is breaking, but the swine is on the rise.
Kid is resilient, but he's got the stars in his eyes.

Victims come in masses, and they leave messes.
The second we let our guard down,
the second they come for our hearts like wolves in hiding,
like the devil they tried to warn us of.

Kill the message before the messenger can talk.
Tell the same lies to keep us in circles.
Keep reaching for the scheming pyramids
that keep us obsessed with fool's gold.

Flying catches and platinum and plastic jubilees,
they're coming for our seconds,
and distracting us with flashy moments to suspend our grief.

Never mind, the Pearl is on detail, eyes moving rapidly as the songstress
calms the dreamers who never learn.
There will be plenty more wounds to lick.

Earth turns, and it burns, but profit margins are key.
Poison kids with chemical spills.
As Lennon said, "smile as you kill."

Nurture over nature, poverty means peers are the law. They're choking
on silver spoons while we fight for a plastic spork.

Be all that you can be, as long as your wealth is absolutely filthy.

Antichrists Prescribe Antidepressants

That single-cell organism has some explaining to do.

Kill the messenger if the punch line is weak.
Savor the texture, since holy water isn't free.

In the middle of the con, I realize being alone is
what we have in common.

Cocktail parties and the who's-who guest list,
I carved my attributes in sand when it was about to rain.

Regrets are just reminders to learn from mistakes.
It's the short-term memory loss that bears the escape.
Still, I can't forget my own and replay them daily, just to keep up with
the reasons for my sins, talking in rhymes to waste time,
and grieving for the loss of solitude.

Take my word, for it's subtle enough to be true.
Take my liver, for it's soaked enough in clear liquid to be used.

Love is only as good as we let it be,
like talk shows and social news feeds,
like the girls who want nothing until they find something, like the tone
of a song that makes it all go away
and lets that single-cell organism get some beauty rest for a change.

Heaven is for Cheap Skates

Shortcut to seeing is ignoring the outtakes,
cancel out the recordings of life's session lessons.
I was raised to be aware, aware of stares.
The real new thing is in retrograde.

Kept the songs so raw, they've ceased aging.
My brain says to vacate these toxic dilemmas,
find new courts to find me guilty in,
kill the sun messenger with sunscreen.

Jesus was Jewish, hence the self-doubting.
Under the stars, I feel like I would anywhere else.
The bottom's up, and the up is left to center, lingering for the sense of
"know-how" to teach me where to find it.

Fill in the blanks of your own life with a dried-out pen.
The secret is pretending not to pretend that you're pretending you
didn't lose yet.

I came here on a wing and a prayer, which means I am too late.
The land of the free, because of vast amounts of unpaid debt.
Land of the lost because the wrong ones found it.
I cheat on the Lord since I am non-fictional.
I crave for my start to have never really happened. I listen to the words
that fill up my background.

Henry was a creep, and his robe was a night light.
Beliefs are the fashion we wear to fool insanity.

You are all alone, but you are not alone there.
Science is religion for smart people.

The less I know, the more I talk in circles.
Had a chance to see it through, but I blinked too quickly.
Lovers of chance are just playing the odds that fate gives a shit.
Distraction is capitalism's biggest seller.
The jig is up; counterculture doesn't have enough to counter. I'm a
lifer when it comes to having no idea what to do next.

Aliens are scared we will lock them in cages.
Sexy talk is for those who love improv.
I see the joining tips in my hips, and I want to cremate my own history.

I leave the silencer on when it comes to my conscience.
The meaning of it all is sealed in liquor.
I need my thoughts to outthink me, willing to get past my past when it
quits reminding me.

I Want to Know Your Favorite Song and What Makes You Cling to It

Smile for me, and I will be its frowning equal sent for me,
but I was lost in dormancy.

Candle dreams of radio lassos, static screams from the draping denial,
sound the schemes of biased trials.

I came from the avenue, and I prayed in the east.
I drank from the devours and got swept up in defeats.

The listening choir is full of hollers while the kingdom lost its come.
I came here for liars but left with civil sensibilities.

Stomach aches from the cleansing; something must pay the toll.

Genius died when the sinister motives strived.
Lost the moment, and the moment is now a stillborn.
Tired stances are dying fences,
and the cult has us on our knees,

just functional-suicidal attempts with pets to please.

The land is loyal to those who step on it.
Lost the summer but gained three more like it.
Salt is the devil, and sweet is God; put them together,
and everyone dies.

My Kingdom Come:
My Will (Power) Be Gone

The Last of the Mohicans is comical to their aggressors.

The Jesus of Hollywood is the epiphany of white privilege.
The sunny side of life is strictly regional.
The poorer the Black man, the more we blame him for his net worth.

I was raised to kiss the brass and kill the empathy,
to whistle mindless tunes and mimic useless fools.

Hair-on-fire constantly sort of mentality.
Kill our ego and go on the right path. Been there, done that.

I canceled the records.
I lost the champagne toast.
I was the last to call mercy.
I was the tempo that never took off.

Short-Term Memory Something

Fill my lines with cutting-edge denials.
Seal my soul with common-tongue trials.

Danger, danger,
Love is as good as it gets.
Savior, savior,
Clean us with constant regrets.

Lend me your ear, and I'll paint you a picture.
Lend me your gaze, and I'll scream it to death.

The look I get from side-jab jobs, the sneer I get violating ancient laws.

Kindred spirits as long as we're soaked in bourbon,
Killing sounds with drumbeats that match our breathing.

The loathing of myself is mutual.
The structure of my heart is whatever shape is hollow.
I can't remember myself when I was me.
So, onward it is with the pretending.

Can't Wait to Get Out of Here

Lost myself in this.
Went too far to see the end, I lost my page,
and can't quite thumb my way out of this one.

Can't you stick your monkey wrenches
in someone else's life for a change?
Trained to mock anything beautiful,
sold to the highest bidder for self-programming.
So, between junkies and saints,
I think I'd rather counsel my own torments.
At least this time, if I'm let down, I will see it coming.

All this muck:
catch a cold, broken nose, heart, and wrist, all in the same blame game.
Making religions out of construction paper and glue, the texture of my
fellow tadpoles mimics starvation for the price of two.

My rebel ideas are past tense - in with the old, out with the new.
Planned a showing of my fondest hours,
but can't focus for those two minutes.
Bold to mold the screaming of heathens that fickle my ideals for the up
and rising cynical peanut gallery.
Hey, you, my losing catchphrase.
I don't have time for your fishermen.
The drones, the doubts, and the scene in which my humility is placed
under microscopes,

I inch my feather-like faith toward your direction,
and when the doors fly shut, the wind will knock it
to the coast of Santa Fe.
Young demons prey the worst. Say what you have to say,
pray your little lives away, don't you ever direct your chants to me.

The scripts that have made our secrets dirty,
why does this longing take so goddamn long?
Don't think of those thoughts.
Don't fear sound.

The snake is a penis, the forbidden fruit is an orgasm.
I take the rain with a frown and
the kicking sensations of no pain, no gain.
Blah blah blah.
The second coming of Christ will be turned into a reality TV program,
where we will all have the chance to pick the sexiest Christ around.

News flash:
white people are the devil.
Condoms are rubber bags with a giant ego.
I cry now to only drink some sort of pure water.
Intense view; the conflict wasn't supposed to grow.
I hate everyone who is not in my view. Boundaries are there to make
sense of the surroundings
that shape our distance to each other.

No one knows the second I triumph; it'll be the collision course
with my diamond-shaped pedigree that is full of hate.
The end of the world as we know it is about the end of Republicans,

and nothing can be created means nothing
is new is the dumb-as-dirt truth.

Yak

Crouching in; pop star breathing, blonde hair, no eyes.
I cry to your headless voice bouncing in.
Counting in 27s until my fate makes sense, pounding in.
Radios should come with filters.
Words are useless, shedding thin.
I wear you like a rosary.
Winter creates want, spring kills off.
I am now allowed to speak on your behalf.
All these years come flooding in. Chords become demon traps.
The words bleach the numbness, full of the sorry syndrome,
entertaining underneath bridges,
and in the dark, where it's harmless, choking on the words
that they didn't have the smarts to say.

Breaking in my assembled tool, winter creates idol's drivel,
put women on the moon.
I owe you my solitude.
February's dawn, April's bloom.

Bouncing in, my attention span
is shorter than my own ambitions.
Yak, yak, yak.

I Hate My Teeth

In a mental race.
Yes, I feel very, very stupid.
I hate my teeth.
Ugly skin, hair is not in use.
Will she smell me coming?
In 2 minutes, wait till they get a load of me.
Bleed now so I won't be a dad.
My, how we don't, don't think at all.

I feel this sorrow in full bloom. Still, I can't put my finger on it.
Ugly seems to be your background.
The demons all bow to you in favor.
Deceitful hearts and deceitful minds, still, I can't put my finger on it.

Raised by a flock of sheep.
Seems best when she's wet.
Sex is dead.
Sex as a gimmick, so kill your idols. Bleed now so I won't be a dad.
My, how we don't, don't think at all.

I feel this sorrow in full bloom. Still, I can't put my finger on it.
Ugly seems to be your background.
And the demons all bow to your favor.
Deceitful hearts and deceitful minds, still, I can't put my finger on it.

Come and Watch Them Multiply

I enchanted these thoughts enough, so here is the blueprint showcase.
I will always throw the first punch,
as long as you're throwing the first insult.
I always aim high.
And, like always, I fall miserably, and each fall is a tender occasion.

I wonder on your being and how the heck you got so far out of reach.
Launching the "I love myself" esteem segments.
But I lost the DNA of my true self.
Now the end of the world seems to be a bed of roses.
Laughed myself to sleep.
Would have cried, but that nonsense action
was numbed out years back.
How can you get even more sad when you don't have anything to lose
to be sad over?

Those days are fiction now.
I walk my garden and flower my water.
Kiss the bees and kill off the little girls who try to sell me sweet nectar,
but are really plotting the chance to put poison in my love chemicals.
So, the infections will devour my only chance
to fall in love with myself.
Blah blah.
You talk too much, you never shut up.
Feverish.
I just want to write the rest of my life out.
Nothing left to say, so I will say it again with new words.

Time is just a fabricated tool to let you sleep at night.
I think the Bible should come with a surgeon's warning.
The first thought that relieves me in the morning is going back to sleep.
I caused too much stress in my own head, and I'm the hell-bound hero
that seeks my own death.
Peel me out, I want out for good this time.

New beat

Will you break my fall?
Make me count on your small talk?
You mimic sweet relief.
It resembles this refuge heart.
I say in my monotone voice of choice,
"You are my life, and I don't want to ever see
another day without you in it."
This is to ease your sense of worry, bring shivers down your spine,
and sighs to your tender side.

New beat, a chance to catch a second breath
and address the latter-day saints,
and focus on more important procedures of the moment.

Fine and dandy, suited for your taste buds.
Webs and the notes that I use to jolt my soul
into a more fulfilling climax.
Wondering if the negative side of my being
will take a lunch break soon.
Can't think straight through all of my self-condemnations.
Inconceivable to fret on these struggles.
I made my own fate
and toast to the seconds I finally am made alive, thanks to you and my
favorite songs.

I am real.
Better believe the hype.

I forgive myself for just as long as I can forget.
Next step is to look at myself in the mirror without disgust.
Until then, kiss me good night and finger my dreams,
cause orgasms of hope.

Heard Things, Little Bit

Pull your own weight and tackle some real issues.
I was gravely misinformed. I blame myself for this.

I'll soon scratch out my options just for another reason to give up.
Can't handle another episode, and I accept this struggle
like it was mine to commit to.
Better off if I were never found.

Yonder on,
I will place more attention on happy thoughts.
I don't know how to just focus on pleasant things.
It is so much easier to waver and let this take its course,
than actually think I am worthy
of your time and compassion.
Can't put my finger on it, and when I do, it bites me,
and the coward that I am falters.

Broken record,
I only speak in echoes and in Simon Says game speech.
Simon says, kill the moment I waste on common thinking.
Played along for so long that the only thing I lost
was the time I could have spent on purposeful living.

I wish there were more to living than what
has just been thrown in the wind.
Wouldn't it make more sense to work for two days and have off five?
Or if everyone was doing what they wanted,
wouldn't life be grander then?

It's like we think we have to suffer to live,
so the more horrible times we have,
the greater the chance to have a better afterlife.

If there is one.
I don't even think there is one.
Well... but then how can that be true?
Nothing is destroyed or new in the universe, so off we go.

But during wake, I feel like I can take on the world, and then the third
hour in, I'm on my knees, craving the older version of me.
Delightful and refusing this test
that is presented only to torture and keep me wanting more.
How long will this take?
How long will I sulk and stare at the glimpse of hope that is dangling
by a teensy-weensy speck of what is my self-esteem?

I wish I would give myself a break.
I wish I were more; I wish I could be beautiful
and always have the perfect thing to say.
I wish I had the courage to be myself.
I wish I could forget those pesky thoughts.
I wish I never found out what it's like
to know what is hard to move on from.
I wish my emptiness came with refills.
I wish the doubts and paranoia were just imaginary.

Forgot my head and the reasons I babble for;
I am not allowed to play with those thoughts.
I am too numb and dead to function. Blah blah blah.

Oil is killing us.

Sonnets Come and Sonnets Grow on Trees

Pop, pop, pop music.

The area known for fewer incidents of rape and acid rain,
the shade is sought in paper births.
The structure of beliefs found in my own worst nightmares
and fever spots that overwhelm.
Can the small talk and the "I love you" sagas, which demand a
refreshed belief pattern.

On to bigger, better agendas of the day.
Blank out the second-hand thoughts.
Better off in some intense hoopla that is full of drama than secret
patterns of trying to get laid and feeling like I was godsent.
I worry too much for me to actually think.

Let the downing of the dumb and foolish sound-effect itself to the
grand toast of a human race that would rather hold its breath
than realize its place in the swing of things.
I hold a candle to the enlightened songs that fill my soul with all that is
worthy to help me find a mate.
Let those who feel most appealing to condemn my attributes
sulk in their ugliness and neglect of life as a large vacation or a place
where everything is where it's supposed to be.
Let go of the images that create wars, boys who are so focused on who
they don't want to be that they never get to be themselves.

Found myself again, where I tripped and lost my car keys.
Most likely not alert enough to see everything
being taken away from me.
The love I want is sitting on the edge of my tongue, of course, next to
the purpose of all this.

Pain is to realize there is a reason for our existence, and it's too risky to
realize the importance or the lack of it.

I am the only figure I role to, baby, baby.
I want to be Elvis
Dead and remembered for my beautiful moments and sideburns.
Help me, my friends.
Help me again.
Don't know if I, being this lonely, is getting me anything.
It better get me a new glimpse and a single solid substance,
or someone to cling my desperation clauses on.
Damn, I hate the truth.
Like my opinion haters, and like the man I'm connected with,
I swallow my ambitions and beg for some more justice,
and more tactics to follow myself for once.
Bleached and boring as can be,
I string these words in a repetitive manner.
Seems to me that the stricter the walls I raise, the harder the day
without regret becomes. Fought my fight and lost my tones with the
one that was supposed to bring them to a higher plane.
Let go of my anger, and I may be forgiven just yet.

Sounds like I'm full of hell and fury.
It's the opposite.

I'm full of the kind of pep that won't release my damaged desires but
fascinates my daring sides,
and creates a conquest for the planet that consumes itself.
A wall of concrete suggestions
that are dealing with the junctions of my position as a child of the
powder's son and the Bible Belt's offspring.

Will you go with your ambitions tomorrow?
Will the stand I create mask itself to
a more particular plane of existence?
Owned space is a joke, like these life packs, and in the jungle, you slip
me your cross, and you rape me of all that is for my liking.
Take your toll, and I will follow.
The rules may never change, but neither will I.
About time I scream out to these ones
who seek my knees to the ground,
and my soul's excuses for why I'm not living.

Well, not for me, I am free.
Just need to fall more in love with my beauty.
That's right, the beauty you have failed at trying to cease.
Letters never sent,
my persuasion is always pretty and clean.

Forever involved with those who know what I know and still have the
beauty to sing about it.
Let me live, and I will do the same for you.

Children, count yourselves as dependents now.
You are going to see why when it's too late.
Alternative and drastic to your limits,

I am never going to feel sorry for you.

Hang your head as low as can be.
You deserve the feelings of this sod's last years.
Tell the truth,
and catch a soul of your own.
You never had control.
Feather my ambitions and water my horizons.
It's my turn for the picking.

Out of Time

The purest blood is secretly dirty.
As innocent as a child, all the warnings too big to believe.
Not one's fault to be so wild.
No one is telling me the truth. I can't live now, I'm too dead.

So, what do all my frustrations prove?
Should have stayed with him instead.
Our time is suicide.
Our days are lost.
Our role models have lied, and we must pay the cost.

I wasn't up to myself.
I didn't mean to be so wrong.
I wanted to be someone else, but I guess I've been dead all along.

My God, why have thou forsaken me?
If there's any justice or love in your body, alone with the fears of how I
die, maybe you could cast a light and set this caged bird free.

Forever has Nothing on Michael Stipe

They used to say I walked tall, and I had the stuffing to prove it,
and that my wings were soaked in sewage,
and I was baffled and bruised before I could have an orgasm.
Just a soundwave I've been dying to hear.
Out come the wolves with their rabid insults and teeth made to pierce
my sensitive coding.
You and the horse you rode in on, back to square one.

Easy to hate yourself and want to die, but the sex on the beaches
and the favorite habitats near warm climates
will only make you feel invincible for so long.

Then you'll wake up in a cold sweat on a Tuesday, in the middle of the
night, with the pounding of reasons,
and conclusions hidden by fear and doubt.
And you will wonder who these people are, and where did the fabric
qualities of innocence go?

The court jester theatrics you display to get a bigger work hole
has replaced your common sense of we are alone.

And in danger of falling out of context: danger, danger, keep contained
with fashion magazines and whose-who-telethon.
Yep, everything is great, and I am just another sap, and I won't think,
no, I won't think, just like you.

Succumbs

Sit around by myself, catch myself in a moment, but I wish I would let it go, flow to the moon and the ends of Jupiter and Saturn, where I will meet you with tea and news of harmony and perfect thoughts.
Beauty seeks a new refuge in you.
I bring the kingdom come and the series of defeats that would make the pope feel insecure.

Evil does what evil feels most evil to do,
and that's the way I make my tools,
and I prove myself every second I choose.
Body is feverish and melting from the exposure.
Chatter the power.
I walk alone as I did in my sleep and the nights before, when the passion was in the rearview, and I wanted all that I wanted.

Yell the message, chin up.
I will be more sound than ever with your touch.
Every level I reveal, my stomach in knots,
love seems to plague but not relieve.
I owe these phases and the gestures to your suffering cause.
The second I awake,
I confuse myself enough to breathe without regret.

Yell with me the meaning of the years I poked myself in the eyes. Time to take my world by the ears, scream the gestures.
Make me feel the passion.

Blah blah blah, just a touch away.
I believe in time as a market for glorified bracelets.

Twins and singing saints, I will be the best I was for the moment.
Shake off my intense demands for more than one glory shot, but in the
seconds that I am good, I fumble it to see that I'd rather sulk before I
splatter my views. I wish I were like a bird and the flying nun.

Yell a blah, blah, blah.
Light is not as strong if you are blind to my point of view.
Find me an excuse that takes my breath away.
Tickle and screams.
I feel better if I never met you.
Not you, but you know those who feel the need to tell me things that
were never supposed to be felt or thought.
I hate myself, and I want to die.
Then, just like that, I'm smiling and can't wait till tomorrow, want to
be a happy sod.
Enough is gibberish.

Running for what was to be a short spree,
but seven years of nonsense has run its part.
I wish to stop this madness,
and speak of nothing that reminds me of such nonsense.

I owe everything to your love.
It broke and awoke me, with peachy-keen textures,
and the easy-to-kill self-esteem in full view.
I have enough,
just want to live as long as I have the chance to do so.

In the morning, I falter,
but at least I'm trying to capture the text of one's journey.
Brave and humble, I stumble the wavelength, and in beauty, I break,
too fearless and willing to sulk
than rather be my own favorite topic.

Wish that the struggle wasn't so intense,
but I fell before it really would have hurt.
Cameras and the altars, one and the same.
Yell me the ingredients it takes to feel this passion constantly.
Music hates you; I don't disagree.
Why would we suffer so much if it wasn't
shifted so preciously in melody?

I walked the enchanted lakes with princes and
the weavers and the song's son.
In the later part of my life, I will owe myself a better song. It's about
time I said I was with me and my point of view.

This kiss blanks out the suffering and
shakes the demons out of my mold.
A chance to be beautiful is all I ask,
and the hand of her and the heart to follow.

Let me out of this, lead me out of the wasteland,
show me the meaning of what was to be blissful,
show me the dreams I have sacrificed all to keep afloat. Prophecy of a
mad boy seeking refuge in these sounds.
Time is only a marketing tool for calendars and morning talk shows.
Let me out of here.
Let's dance the talk away.

California and the Memphis blues,
I will meet you there and take the world by storm,
from enough messages to actually make sense.

I feel alone, numb, and confused, willing to set this on its right tone,
feather-like faith, dreaming of my only chance to be your love.

Sin, gin ta te.
I am about to explode, to Haiti and the small towns of England.
Come and take me away.
Forever will never be as remarkable as you.

Snatch

The sky is falling.
The pope and the president have jumped everyone's bones.
I break the cycle to see that gravity will always prevail.

Note to self: the bigger they are, the faster you run.
Let's go to the land of dreams and happy flings.
Wish memories were more like the digestive system, keep the ones that
are good for you and that you need nutrients from.
Get rid of the wasteful kind that circles around your head,
and seems to hold your breath, even when you don't want to.

Fall on me if you must.
Drive the polluted metal-moving devices,
eat the other species to feel more like God,
have sex to feel more like God,
create so you can be just like God.

I buy and sell that which was never mine to begin with.
The young lady has, for so long now, been in need of a heart transplant.
Kids must be born with magnets in their brains;
they seem to fall right into the metal traps.
Never mind the metal ones, I'm more concerned
about the mental ones.

Lipstick is just a mask for your true intentions,
lipstick and the lies you built to protect and flaunt.

Brave new world, sail me a new ambition period.
Play the "what the hell" games till dawn.

The needles are in full demand,
so are the rubber bags, the dramatic motives,
and the pop killers too.

The sky is falling; looks sort of like Swiss cheese.
Ice is melting, going to need new swimming trunks, or buy a bubble to
live in where I will decorate it with pictures of pictures
that resemble outside.
Would go out for the real feel, but too afraid of the scene.
Magic powder is claiming more than Jesus can. Liquids and plants
seem to make more sense than they should.
Blame the world for these mistakes.
I owe nothing to you, and you know it.

I will come out of the woodwork and devour all that stands in my way.
Live through moment by moment in a torture-myself mindset.
All I know and learn came from your crosses and lower-class labels.
Go back in time so I can kill you now and watch it with a grin,
over and over again.

Thank you, my good friends, fiends or what have you.
I've done all I can, and you still have the balls to mock.
Self-doubt and self-loathing are my superpowers, but at least I'm not as
ugly as you've become.

My own bushwhacked mind is going to give you lip,
the finger, and above all, hell.

I will give you all hell, left with self-hatred and a desire to hurt, with hope I will feel resolved, but all that comes is more reasons to self-doubt and loathe.

Helmet for my brain, words for my soul.

I will protect myself from all that oppose, including bushes, ogres, and girls that squirm and squeeze out lies.

I am done. I am a riot.

I want to live it up and give my regards to Henry for this gift.

Losing My Religion

I've Got a Bad feeling About This One

Yell a little louder so we can ignore you with all our might.
Things that bite, things that frighten me all night.
This is a joke if you don't get it, but it's gospel for those who do.

These Christians sure are holy.
'Tis the reason you can see right through them, including the lies that
mimic the false cries. You are all alone without yourselves.

Does it mean I'm homosexual when I know when I look good?
I'm so in love with myself, does it mean I caught the gay?
Too scared to look at my penis, might get excited
when it's bigger than I thought.

I stand alone on what I've learned from TV
and self-help books.

Deck the halls with the lower class and cast T's.
This man in the box is fantasizing about your sins.
If money is not only a man-made concept but also the root of all evil,
then why is paradise made of streets of gold?
Why does this infinite creator sit, and why does it sit on the throne?
The stranger the fiction, the more they buy.
And if God is he, how big is his penis?
Does he masturbate, and when he does, what does he do it to?
And more importantly, does he use a condom when he fucks?
Because if he created STDs, he should have to play by the rules too.

Wouldn't it make more sense to see God as having boy and girl parts?
A masculine and feminine voice, with breasts
and a 12-inch member.

If God is a hermaphrodite,
does this mean transgenders are the chosen people?
And does it mean that God is gay
when he made the image of the perfect man?
How does God know what women like unless,
hmmm . . .
Yell a little louder, I didn't quite catch the meaning
of life this time around.
But the statues you provided and the paper lives
we abide by are ending soon.

Too much thinking for this hour.
Come back when we've got the answer for . . .
for life, love, sex, death, hate,
penis envy, coffee, French kissing, the love for small animals, and the
existence of breast implants.

Hell is on Fire, and Heaven is Too Wet to Camp at

Jesus was carved out of white imagination.
Noah was the original incest creator.
David killed his best friend to get laid. Job was
God's most obvious ego trip.

Samson was too gullible to have long hair.
Lucifer was doing what God made him for.
The only thing Moses got for being a "yes man"
was being thrown out of the promised land.

The original sin was when God made it. God's extortion is its
superpower. Jesus is the reason for the season,
which means it's his fucking fault.

Abraham's schizophrenia almost did Isaac in.
Jacob was a conman, even to his own kin.
Joseph's coat of many colors was ugly as sin.
Moses saw a fiery bush when the shrooms kicked in.

All the gospels were gossiping a generation too late,
hearsay and hand-me-down tales to pollute.

Entropy

Further adventures of the blame mascot.
Prey, pray, what have you?
Achtung, don't have any more cheeks to turn, so watch that tongue of
yours, or I will focus on your faults for a change.
Hope you choke on that silver spoon.
Think you point so much to excuse your manhood.
Let me think about these notions...
You plead to a ghost and bow to minerals.
Worship the flag, but only when under attack,
and swallow all they sugar-coat for you.
Tisk, tisk.
Never direct your isolations on me.

Tell the lambs I'd rather tell tales than practice dead rituals.
Skyscrapers are just tributes to manhood.
Christianity can be easily excused as schizophrenia.
Chemicals wouldn't be so imbalanced if Jesus did his job for once.

I yell too much.
I wish to find a sequence of rituals that doesn't leave so much guilt.
If life sucks, we die and all that shite,
why can't Christmas be every day,
and we have one day of being awful to each other?

We will call it the Bizzaro Christmas,
but this one will actually make sense
and have a purpose besides selling overpriced merchandise.

It won't be just to forget the year is over,
and you have a few regrets.
Wish it weren't so easy to worry.
Smiles are like wallpaper these days.

I found my tongue in handcuffs again.
Slipped through the cracks and broke myself open.
The stitches rip open every time I stare or sigh.
Guess it's time I prey too.
I found I am less than ordinary, but too close for comfort.

Racecar backwards is still racecar, the same as your cult-like religion,
no matter how you explain it.
Do me a favor and explain it in sign language
so I can poke myself in the eyes
and ignore you for a few moments more.

Get some peace and rest,
and maybe really find out what Jesus had in mind.

Lyrics From a Song

I know how it's going to be.
Psalms, Proverbs, and Ecclesiastes.
None of this is making sense; I should have gone with Buddha instead.

"I'll be watching you, and I'll be stalking you,
and I'll never be alone again."

All these things taking place, not my idea of saving face.
Girls who can't afford the pill, hope coat hangers have refills.
"I'll be watching you, and I'll be stalking you,
and I'll never be alone again."

You, whom I feel close to me, cancel out my negative needs.
All this to lend a hand,
I failed, and now you're dead.
Now nonsense means love to me.

"I'll be watching you, and I'll be stalking you,
and I'll never be alone again."

Soma, I Rot

This, in due time, will show its purpose.
Will it be the death or the triumph of a lifetime?
She is the kind I would like to wear around the world, show her as my
soul's match; not another would be as beautiful.

So, I deceive my guards some more,
and I pretend that she is not in control.
I am full of this misery that claims us both.
I drink proper fluids to tame the beast.
My only pride and joy is in her name now;
'tis the reason for the demands of this child's dreams.
I will only kiss my thoughts of you. I can't know what it is not to know.
I hate my mouth; I hate my tongue.
It has failed me once again.
Can't quite get the right slogans,
and I will choke before I say how I really feel.

You break me down with your eyes, caught in this whirlpool of feelings
that I fall in love with.
Forget me not, my love.
I am still singing in the corner,
waiting for the dream to dream itself alive.
I am offering you my everything.
Isn't much, but it may keep you loved.
This is it, my pledge and creed.
I am to cease all human contact if you don't walk with me,
become a hermit in North Dakota,

raise a family of goats and possums,
name them Penelope, Icicle, and George.

We will sit around singing songs about faith and love,
and of course, the lack thereof.
If you would like to take a peek, or maybe to move in and raise your
own goats, just follow my trail of words that
will always be connected to you.

Bored in the USA

Oligarchy Orcs on the March

Space travel over yacht travel, health care over bomb scares,
windmills over oil spills,
scientific insight over the Christian right.

This is the weight of the world.
It'll sink any day now, like parts of the California coast,
like the moral fiber of the West.

Yelling at echoes, swelling of egos,
selling greed shows,
telling lies at a new low.

Beheading of court jesters, rooftop bullies running amok,
faceless men ruling the land. The future never happened.

Cruelty on a power spree, apathy to get some sleep,
numb from the days on repeat, ice-cold behavior; silent defeats.
Stubborn hearts are to blame, as are those seeking hollow fame.
Count your pennies as they count their silver spoon dollars.
The revolution will not be live-streamed.

Oligarchy orcs on the march, raising capital gains as common pockets
drain, raping the skies and soil,
buying speech to fool the follies,
and prepping for the inevitable end to the land of
make-believe tyranny.

KKK

K
I'm not like that.
K
You are too small to speak.
K
Shall it be your failed agenda?

Before you slander, I think it's time I pull you
a seat and buy you a drink.
Whatever you like, as long as it shuts you up for a second or two.

Parade in your costumes and display the 20th letter as your salvation.
Count the mistakes you make.
It seems I'd have to start in 1890 and freeze myself
for the next 178 years
to keep up with all that you think.
It must take a lot of rapes to get your mind off of it.

The day I see a Black, non-Christian woman as president . . . sigh.
Silence is the best medicine in your case.
So, take the robe and your dirty sheets, tell your clan and cronies
to ask your Jewish, dark-skinned lord for forgiveness.

It's time to return to the trailer parks. Hate your TV,
not the beautiful sons of slaves and civil leaders.
Martin, X, the power of the soul and rhythm.
You don't stand a chance.
Hide behind your mask, pray for forgiveness for the last 150 years.

You may be able to look at mirrors
as you pass through your pointless life.

K

Hitler was a sociopath.
K
Your white sheets and pointy hats make you look like a tampon.
K
Don't take yourself too seriously, 'cause we think you are a joke.

Propaganda: symbols for stupidity,
and your thoughts will only hold you back from growth.
If a Black man has the same blood type,
plays your favorite sport, leads your armies,
has something to say that's worth listening to, what will you do then?
Take your number and wait in the backyard
of your attempts to get back to Europe.
No one is holding you here.
Blonde hair and blue eyes are deficiencies.
Life began with those you despise, and the more you push and hate,
the more they and I will push back,
till you are condensed to a life that you pursue for them.

Separation from your stupidity is a win for all.
Or at least, catch a cold or cancer and die off.

Us vs Them

They zapped me in, fell asleep, but still no remorse.
Can't outwit it, so off I go to Planet 9, where I mark my horizons
and talk dirty to my saint split personalities.
Feel more alive when faced with this approach.
You are the talk of the town and the crimson tide,
the stinging that doesn't keep the feelings in swing.

Take the torch and light the glass pipes, filled to the brim with
nonsense and thoughts I never claimed.
With all this pressure, I still rewind every
lacking moment to clear my name,
to make sense of the fact I let myself do that to myself,
and commit myself to more important segments.

Telling you how I felt when I made more sense, to keep you in touch
with the burning. I will capture the temptation
and sell it to the modest hearts.
Spend now what is at your fingertips; tomorrow will bring you another
vial of pitfalls with only an ounce of relief.
Easy to sing along when you are sad,
harder when the luxury has passed.
Wasn't the pursuit I bargained for.
This fortune is under the panel.
I walk to the river when I should have taken a jet ski.

I wonder on the poisons I inhaled.
I ponder on thoughts that can be disregarded.
I am silk, I am soil. I will run the mile.

Dance the demons to a happier place.
Then they will bow, blow, and leave me be.
People lack the courage of prime.
I run like that coward I was raised to be.

Forbidden.
All the priests are your pedophiles, and all the planes now bring shivers.
And all the sounds are too hollow to bounce off your ears.
And the lack of imagination plagues us, this daily bread.
And the beacons are dim from the waste of energy on the cycles of war.
And the day I was alarmed, it was too early
for me to care but too late to fear.
I guess the high will take a shortcut back to my center.
Watching the buildings fall with high hopes, and the boys and girls
have no beanstalks.
And the church and state were never separated.

Explains why women will never be ahead.
And that most sex is still wrong.
And how anything different is stoned with words that are as bad as
sticks and stones.

No fear walking up to my end's rope.
We all feel like the pits.
Leaving it all behind, the drum has been beaten.
This life is full of imitation and plastic castles.
Too late for redecorating.

Let's return to Saturn and hope,
trying to keep a view.

Yell a little louder.
I can't stand it when it takes my heart like that.
Dreading what's next is my superpower.
Power to my wavelength, those who know what I know, sign up for the
yellow, red, and green.
I will begin a new beginning.

Born to live and die in touch, just a touch of hmm of what I believe.
I believe in lengths, and it's time to take my medicine.

Been there, done that, lacking the links to my present self.
Sometimes I panic and raise my blood pressure, and the chemicals may
go out of balance,
and then, just when the usual thoughts presume, I will hear the notes
sent by those who know better than any other.
And my day has come to its peak.
Prime living and the way we go . . .

How to Get Rid of
Man Boobs, Obama?

Time is just an excuse for me to be formatted. I am alone in this
glimpse of when I think I'm making sense.
Here I stand in quicksand again, relishing in semi-accomplishments,
thinking in circles, so I become dizzy enough to forget my conscience.

In the mind of one who is forever in debt to paranoid pollutions,
intrigued by those who know the cost of ridiculous conclusions.
Wish they'd tell me how to cast the demons to bay, cash my tunes in,
and live in constant humanity.

Where I will spend not only my life,
but also the currencies that have claimed it in full.
Senate votes and presidential poses, the poor can be called poorer,
and the rich can still be called dicks.
The money it takes to bail out your parachutes can fund enough
welfare to put Jesus to rest.
The killing excuse they use.
The willing of the poor and abused.
The pawns to the rich man's war,
the teenage sons that will never be more.
Trade and sell, but we will never be free.
Insiders betray with speculators' greed.
Live without caution, the government's in control, then it's filed under
mishandled, and neither house is at fault.

The bluest bloods keep standing tall,
while the silver spoon kids make laws.
Thank God, the only ones to suffer now are the ones
who are used to it by now, but anyhow . . .

Yell Some More

Feeling quite out loud, pounding in my superstitions. Walking to the
last of my coherent segments, tell the truth and feel raped.
I walked the temple, and I saw the holes worthy of the snow,
like happy trails.

Runaway so far that I think I've gone in circles, and phew,
finally home is yonder near.
Will the forecast call for the land to be raped some more?
Fall on this and that,
quote the Bible and the politicians who seem to lie the most sincerely.

Full of my own worst thoughts to ever ponder on the tragedies
of the molecules wasted for your existence,
the week ends like it should always.
The pounding of my fist against my head, in the same rhythm as your
bitter attacks from the cloudiest of minds, belittles me.
Alone forever, this is to be my favorite target, to fling my righteousness
and attempts to be the sacred heart orgasm.

Sex is a fleeting distraction, and I have no time to display my attention
span on your mindset's assets.
Kaleidoscopes of feta cheese and the true reason
why saints become saints
(they give better head).

Temper, temper, God.
Use your tools of the TV, the flag, the green, and prey more on the fear.

God is no more a man, as the pinpoint of my discussion is excused by
those who oppose it. I love sounds, and they seem to be more of God
than your book and jewelry that are so designed to scare and taunt.

Give us this, our daily bread, and then tomorrow go excuse the priest
touching the Prozac junkie holy rollers of tomorrow.
Instead, why don't you get the bread, go to Afghanistan, Ethiopia,
Taiwan, Detroit, your neighbor's house, or whoever needs the carbs.
Wellness is in doubt, and suffering is intensely the progress that seems
to be well sedated from normal agendas.

I know the problems that seem to be faced by the poor, low, lower,
even down lower, so low that everyone seems
not to see and seems to forget about,
or "think absent sight, absent mind" class, and the needles are claimed
to have more use than the baseballs and fishing poles,
and how this life leads you to a higher power to cling to,
but instead, you cling to a wire-for-hire puppet show
that stings and strips away all that could have been worthy of thinking
of.
Blah blah blah.

And also, I recall the hurt of the hungry, the cold,
and that pointless feeling that you are worthless.
Even after this, you develop this stinging of your own
that seeks only to devour your self-love,
and make you seek the wisdom of the ones that lack the depth of
despair, and the feeling that there is more to this
than meets the eye and soul.
And then you start to dwell on those parts that stung deep. You feel like
you want to go over it as many times as it takes to feel resolved,

or the feeling like you didn't let that just happen,
that you had control all along.
I fake this tongue-in-cheek program, tune in, and falter to my madness.
Lack of energy and lack of admittance of truth will never shackle me to
their disgust. Living forever is not my agenda;
just to be young as long as I can.

My motivations lie in my quest to be the greatest human
I possibly can come to be,
and at the same time, I want to stay that way and
not fall down to their expectations,
because they want me to feel like I was born to die like them,
alone and a waste.

Yelling in any sound formation to kill my temper villains and further
my days as a vessel for the beauty that I would, and I will,
and am now dying for.
I believe this journey can't quite focus its grip on my views till I first
lasso my attempts on my own self-gratitude.
Enough about me . . .
What do you think about me?
Feverish and yellow from holding my breath till these polluted
thoughts leave the oxygen that I live by.
Don't want to have those thoughts in my head when I breathe, can't let
God think I'm accepting this as living.
I nearly live.
I break the second I hear the words that sink me to the boy I flee from.

Brought to you by the demons that have this down pat, the ones that
want me to dwell on those pesky thoughts I've mentioned.

Mondays I feel the most alert, but by the next day, I find my draining
process incoherent to my struggles.

Yes, I know I am the bearer of my own worries. Tell me something that
actually helps and makes me fall into your rhythm.
Don't like the followers of your kind,
and the people that follow your gold and green.
I know the basic context,
and I ache every time I am not intensely in love with my view.
Drastic measures, selling of my concepts,
willing to trade the ability to eat and laugh it all away
for an ounce of truth.
I'm not scared anymore.
I am just scared of what I really think of myself.
I run around in these patterns,
and I laugh, hate, cry with, make fun of,
and love and devour myself constantly.

Can't help that it mimics the struggles of
Darwin's 15 minutes and Marx's working suggestions.
Too much TV and the mixture of powder and saints have left me in
touch with my love for songs and heart-shaped dreamboats that sell my
heart out every time I feel the foolish thoughts of how I might have
found the one warm spot that reminds me of the ever-constant
changing, supreme, beautiful, drastic, and constituently perfect
formation of what is close to love and God.

Yell some more.

Brave New Blah Blah . . .

I changed the locks but left the keys in your possession.
Owe me an apology, so here it goes:
Regret never seems so bittersweet, change never was an issue.
Punk rock phonies make me sick,
legends of a decade to sell you products,
to place you back in your fondest moments.

Love seems it was left out in the water too long, pruned up, and can't
quite catch his own breath.
Put it in the oven and bake it to your liking, well done, worn out,
or in pieces for everyone to share.
That seems to be the treasure hunt.
Catch a cold, a crisis, and a reason to stay adaptive.

Kept whistling my tunes, dwelling on my more upbeat,
swinging moods.
Dreams never encounter so much negativity formed
by your own doubts.
Run for the hills, and then when you have reached the tippy top,
build a rocket ship and go to the highest planet available.
There, make yourself a little pad that is doubt and debt free.
There you will be without past regret and fear, but there you probably
won't have cable TV, cappuccinos,
and the experiences that seem to explain
so much of why you're demanding more of what you're running from.

Favorite sins made into a sitcom.
The younger the piper, the faster we follow.
Blame the reasons on those you can beat.
The faster the saga goes, the better the chance to get some sleep.

Explanation for a life in constant struggles, found only in rhythms and
melodies that sparkle oh so well. Halt to your condemnations.

I will rescue love when I get my share.
Smarts and the kindred feel that I won't die so alone.
I will talk to you like you are listening.
Chanted too much last night, and now it's become a habit of talking to
myself whenever the feeling provokes.
I'm sipping on the words spoken when I had the heart to listen
without doubts.
I have a tale to tell,
yet I bite my tongue in fear I may be right.
King of all I see, one day further,
I am made humble in my defeats.
I am alone with nowhere to go.
Hit the deck and get the drama out of my head.
I believe in love as an abstract and as a market
for sappy movies and songs
that I never wanted to feel in the first place,
and the campaigning for the regret
of feeling this free, and this wise, and this great.
I will break before I fall, and I will spit out the lies you planted
and squeeze out the poisonous doubts you drove in.
Help me get this fever out and kick me when I'm down.
So, it goes . . .

Who am I speaking of? Why am I running from it?
The principal is stuck, and the wondering of it all is plucked,
and I am alone like I began.
That's me punished, that's me laughing it up, up to my end's rope.
Let me get the show off, and I promise you, love, upon all that is sure
of and true and beautiful.
I swear, love, I break every time you decide to flee in a rush, leave me in
the dust with no further notice or a message
from a divine intervention.
I swallow you whole.
Hope to get the moment-by-moment playback of your triumphant
return, 'cause it's about time you come back where you belong, in the
passions that I require,
and, of course, in the life of a boy
whose only demand has been to cast lights
and drive hearts to want more.

Most of all, he wants love to be stapled to his lungs,
seeing the importance of both as equal.
Endure, and I will conquer all in our way, love.

Doge This

The league of voters kept their voices muted.
What followed were their screams of regret, with denial infused.

Clown wisdom from clown pretenders,
the joke lacks humor since it's on us.
Worms and decayed brain cells.
The browner you are, the more cells they have to sell.

Regulate the x-man, regulate the cash flow,
regulate the means that give them control.

Lesser men are getting more, while the wiser men are ignored. This is
the way of the world, said by those who rigged it.

Delete the media if it doesn't echo the narrative that keeps you feeling
secure that strong men are out for you,
even when they're hollowed through.
That silver spoon babies aren't just salesmen, that dyed blonde hair is
part of the job description, that it's okay to waste as long as they profit,
that the pocket change you get is equal to their billions.
We count on our hands how many times this happened.
Ran out of fingers, and to the toes we go, counting how many piggies
are next to choke.

The wayward games only they can win.
Loyalty hires for this constant grift, roaring back its ugly head,
just in time for the depression to kick in.

Love is Blindness

Okay Hill

Wasted a million moments to find ways
to occupy the next few to come.
The less I know of these sticky situations,
the cleaner my wings will be in the long run.

As I settle for my prison cell with a view,
lack of intuition has branded me a fool.
Careful heart, but I have clumsy feelings that tend
to tread in areas that are forbidden.

As pretty words from pretty girls cure what ails you.
You see, now to let yourself down is best to spark nostalgia.

Turpentine and candlelight let me know what I'm in for.
I stare too long from afar,
'cause I can't get enough of your beauty.

Sarah is Great and I Love Her, Silly Rabbits

In my affections, alter my perfections.
I save my hallelujahs and bathe in the moonlight. I am renewed.

Just the touch I am in need of, in your wave and in your cravings.
I find myself deeply notched in your haven.
I want to let the sorrows fade away to Nebraska, in genocides and
multiple dead-end case studies.
I find out that the battles were just hobbies.
I pass the time till I kiss your neck.

Have you seen the cattle call? Is it time to fall asleep in me?
You and I find ways to play hide and seek, then
0492834209840928382839849389 minutes in heaven.

You focus on simple and drivel minds,
the way it feels to be in the right 24/7.
I am impressed, and I am impossible.
I dust off my demons and whistle sweet somethings in your view.
Tries and cries and the window of divine lives.
I was just in the lust of another touch from you.
Your lips are soft, full of passion.
I feel it now.
The intense and numbing familiarity in my heart, in my thoughts, and
in my memory bank.

There is our embrace; it keeps the wolves at the door,
kissing salsa and drinking lemons.

Bravery is fluorescent in my facial expressions.
I'm not sure how this is going.
Not as good as my 2,667 thoughts and expressions.
Feed me your desires, let me in.

I want to know you in detail.
What are your favorites, and what is too hard to take?
Beautiful is your way, and those kisses remind me to stay alert.
A happy day is coming when you take your place next to mine.
My glow is seen from outer space, the moons of Saturn.
It starts with my eyeballs, through my abs, and my toes too.

Dreams of kisses and holding hands,
years of trying to find out where I want to put my lips.
I see you in a way that nobody will ever understand. Follow you in, and
I will transform myself again.

Drama and decisions, triangle of twisted intentions,
titles of our lifetime movie.
Whistling to the tunes of my doubts, carving my dreams into your
stone-like stubborn way.
I am just an insult; the right thing for you.
Back and forth, blah blah blah.

No sugar and spices, condiments taken away from true meanings.
So, order up some more of that salsa, and we will make the day our
own private Wyoming.

All the Love in My Heart

...And another one kicks and screams.
Off she goes to the land of good and plenty,
with her ambitions in demand
and her lips syncing wherever it works.
The tale of two scorned lovers from the womb.
He, the poor one of some sort, she keeps her silver spoon well handy.
He trips and falls his way onward;
she hums and skips on her delightful way.
He aches and stares at the cold spots,
the kind we push away or run away from.

She smells like roses, like the essence of a dream.
He rots of beer and the scent of nothing to believe in.

Fingers touch the face.
He begins to speak of the bliss, but words are useless to conduct a
proper account.
She whistles the sweetest songs one could ever hear.

Her eyes pour out a soul not yet scorned, her desires placed on her face,
letting the boy know he can rest from the day's defeat.
She provides the right mood with her smile, nectar this sweet found in
no other realm.

Love getting stronger, enough to claim itself.

Nothing to bring it to a halt, not a building of the not-so-holy, not the
ignorance that fools proclaim gospel.

Yet the struggle rattles on, stripped away from this beautiful moment,
afraid of being fearful and alone.
She cries too much to see the truth tattooed on her mind.
This isn't enough to damage the boy's ego, but it does a number on his
heart and soul.

Boy sinks low enough to ignore her disappearance.
She cries and cries till nothing happens.
Both numb and confused,
they waver, kiss the next cloud of beautiful moments goodbye.

Attempts to reconcile and count the misery, kissing in corners and
shadows so they won't be caught.
Songs keep her in mind and soothe her to sleep.
Nothing could prepare them for what was to come next.
Breakdowns.
The melting of good and evil, the burdens and the muck of time,
too much to keep up with, so run, it is.

Both to the opposite directions, emotionless scandals, the countless
numbers of semi-loves,
never enough to keep their feelings detained,
till the day they ran back into each other's arms.

Kiss the moment, make love to the electricity in the air,
talk about life as one,
and how the world will follow.

Unsure heart leaves girl in doubt, boy still lingering after all these years,
goes to touch to make amends.
Not this time, will have to go to the limits instead.

Tell her all he knows and how it affects her.
Her emotions gone out the window, she turns and leaves it like it is,
empty, and the boy is left in withdrawal.
The air seemed thick that morning.
She excused herself from his attention span.
Dreams they had still surfaced in his way of life.
Her face painted on his memory banks
to keep as a model or sample of God.
They seek comfort in others, but never found,
just sleeping till his heart is hers again.
After all this time, the boy pledges all of his worth to the girl who gave
it to him from the start.

For your own self-gratitude, to the wavelength they could still be,
to the tasks ahead, I acknowledge you. I desire, and I still fall in love
with you every second I get to remember you.

Boy spits, yells, and curses up a storm.
Seems it has returned to the beginning. Poor boy, still poor, wishes for
silver spoons, delightful tunes,
and the girl who possesses all of the above.

So, What More Can I Say?

I will always be this way:
Guessing in the rhythms of my chemically imbalanced heart.
I will ache the rest of the waking days with remorse that I didn't come
clean sooner.

The younger version of me would have whisked you to
North Dakota,
where we would raise cattle, but not for devouring.
And after the harvest, we would make the days to our liking,
with milkmaids and window pies blossoming.
Christmas at Mom and Pop's.
Fourth of July, home on the range.

Back to reality.
In the coldest of hearts, the confusion takes its toll on you,
filling up on frustrations. Here is the release:

The kindest of egos will always mouth the words you pursue.
The checkpoint to happiness, I will make you my happiness,
with sugar blossoms and candy-coded words.
The center of my universe, the interactions I call home.
The dwelling in past regressions, no longer a medium. With the scent
of your realization that you already know what to do.
Signs are simple, and the awakening in your soul is complex, but a
beautiful ritual, I may say.

Cease the confusion with the sweetest dreams,
like window shopping in Paris,
or kissing under the lights of JCPenney's.
I thought of you only 99% of the time.

Don't want to come off too strong.
Instead, I will say that I want nothing else now
but to hold your hand in public,
kiss you underneath the lights of a JCPenney's in Paris,
dance with you to love songs from the '80s.

Intentions are of the purest kind,
with my heart out and about, its toe-curling,
yearning for aspiration, to cease the bewilderment.
I will be in love with you for as long as you let me.
So, never say when.

The Worst Kind of Love Story

Besides the struggles and wannabe thugs,
I am at least the master of my situation.
Besides my tongue that sparkles and haunts,
I am more intense than my feverish reputation.
Besides that ongoing nonsense of hormones of lonely girls, I will move
closer to you to halt your kingdom come.

Wet my lips and pour pity on my lonesome gestures.
Sing to sleep my life away in big beds and bigger drama sessions.
I will lock on to your lips and suck your eyes if it seems profitable.

Never mind the jibber-jabber, I have only come for one reason:
to tell the skeptics to give someone else a chance to be doubted.
Painful as it sounds, I lost myself again.

I hate myself for you,
and I will do it better this time, I swear.
West of the denial, the secrets I have found in an anti-optimistic pile, I
lower my esteem to fit your flaws.
Perhaps this combo will prove how you are too good for me now.
Life can get a little weary and neglected of what it's supposed to be.
Life has an identity crisis and is not the spokesperson of excitement it's
supposed to be.
Life sells itself, you know.

It paralyzes your conscience.
It plays games like hide and seek with your true intentions.

It holds your arms down and wags the riches of the land,
pretending it's within your reach.

What would it do if I were to feel like
I was supposed to when I wasn't so torn?
My torment is ridiculous. It is embarrassing to let myself take
advantage of myself.
I have had too much of it, and here it goes:
Self, time you back off and pick on someone your own size, or at least
maturity level.

Details are my defense.
I hate it when it makes sense to be horrible.
Yet I still carry these burdens.
Nothing will save me now. I guess I'm through.
Exhaled that junk, and with the first breath I inhale,
I am brought to a Ben-Hur stance.
I awake,
pick and point out the misery caused by those who have the nerve to
think negative thoughts about me.

Whatever you need is my religion.
Losing it is my specialty,
and pondering on my mistakes, that's my occupation.
Welcome. You are.
The seasons are dry and bitter if you are on my bad side. So, get off my
tongue and let my sentences run you down for a while.
My feelings are neglected and on strike.
I am still alive, just forgot how to focus.

Approaching demon domains.

I am a rest stop for negative thoughts, so go to the next sap.
Had too much with second doubts, let alone 340321757872 of them.
See you on the bright side, perhaps in another mass of matter.

I Saw the Face of Beauty and it Made me Shiver

The ghost of her, vibrant as ever.
She makes it hard to move on.
I cast my desire away for comfort and ease.
Like laws that only benefit the lawmakers,
I looked for it and cowardly ran when I found it.
The confessions are dim, and my reason is selfish at best.

I ramble like a mammal, and I speak like a freak.
Forgive me for my wandering tongue.
It craves ears to find its relief.

The following is just another attempt to be believable.
Cared enough to justify the lust, and reason is always equal to touch.
I want those eyes to focus kindly on me, see my flaws,
and still be able to stare away.

Just in time to keep me from my mind, conflicted in general, now it's
in its prime. Found your smile in the crowd of frowns.
"If it happens, it happens," is all you allow.
Went to the lengths and tethered my senses, dressed the moment with
appropriate sentiments.
Found the cause and let it take me further,
to a place where you and I will be valued.

Humming

I kiss you on the mouth,
catch myself for two seconds before the doubt
trembles in and out of you.
Through my tongue and blame, I devour the pursuit. Bang.

Take my name and show me what you've got.
I am alone for more than a healthy amount of time.
Yet my whistles tune, and my heart plays hard to get, till my monsters
are cloned into baby monsters, easy to control and less of a mess.

I looked for the crush everywhere.
King of laughter, I ran for the money and the sincere holidays.
I need another chance, even five, if you can spare, to make this
foundation stable again. I belong to this, so let me in.

Let me caress the dreams, what you need.
You and your desert-talk frighten me. I envy your dilemma and
worship the solitude you claim.
Easy to hold on to your beauty if you've never lost it.
In your case, you never did.
So, good going, my beautiful one.
I am yours for the slaying.
Kissing you on the mouth,
stars, calls, the circus of continued negative thoughts.

The time it takes to get back where you belong, all I want, all I need.
The shackles of this youth, ironic supplements that keep us aboard.
Currency is never the strangest.

Let me kiss you on the mouth some more.
Your beauty is permanent.

85

People Need People

Beginning of my triumph, lover, don't leave so fast.
Whistle me a tune, lend me your view so
I can rest from my tainted one.
Breathing never seemed so important; life wasn't my favorite substance.
Finally getting what seems to be justice,
I loathe myself without trying to see why.

My mind is yours for the picking.
Rearrange it and capture its worth.
Attention span set on your every move -
thoughts might as well be yours, as they are all about you.
Not much else to pledge addiction to;
these fingers were meant to pleasure you.
My words didn't matter (until used to praise you).

I long to embrace you, waste only what isn't necessary,
shape our world to our standards,
pull off the way-too-cool-for-you act.

Wink and nod to all those who understand all too well:
I have always longed for this embrace.
It's the striking thoughts I cling to
in order to cleanse your body with my tongue.
My beauty is set to make love to yours.

Caught my tongue, satisfied my intentions.
Lost my dreams for a second, but captured the ones worth the while,
the ones that linger with the scent of you.

Into the Arms of Love

Stalk my haunts, twinkle my nostalgia, favor my good feeling,
seeing as the rest are crippled or paralyzed.

Look over there, here comes another dry spill.
It will cancel my happy sessions and bring the order of demon
appearances that can top all horror tales.

The last time I fell flat on my face. It is a ritual of some sort.
I will break free at 10:32 and sell myself out by 11:12.
I am sold out, drained out, and numbed from guilt too many times to
claim my own nature as past tense.

You are my favorite signature of life.
Tell me by which type you want to free yourself, and I will do it.
Find yourself in a rut,
find your days twisting and curving into each other, like one long,
depressing, epic, disgusting display of life.
Found the seconds it takes to be alive again, arranged my fossil fuels to
last for a few more years, but can't say the same about love. My want
taunts your haunt.

Help me save the world. Play music well into my eighties,
and sell the process and triumphs of my bleeding heart.
You have once again found your way in.
You dazzled and danced to your liking in my head.
I love when you look like that. Count your blessings.

Found out that it wastes more energy
to hate and defend that which has
no significance than it takes to just love yourself,
which is more of a pleasant afternoon, if you ask me.
Hey now,
what is it that you wish to live by?
Are you the kind that will fill me with high hopes
to leave the world pecking away?

I am tired of believing the world is in self-destruction mode,
that hope has been raped,
that the wolves are at our feet,
that all my worries are facts,
that my words will never have impact, that my gestures are forsaken,
and my laughter is in vain.

I am here to shove away those thoughts
from you and kiss you if you need me to,
and maybe the struggle can take a backseat,
and we will tumble our way to something better.

"D" Section of the Dictionary

Now...

I want to bathe her in a pool of beer, so she will not only taste great but get me drunk too.
I would love to look at her for hours and cleanse my wings with her beauty. I sulk and sink as I see her walk away.

How many fates turn around in mid backstroke?
Say you want me, and I will be yours for the taking. Me, I'm tired, and I want to sleep inside you.
You, whom I desire more than food, water, and wine.
Would love to play with your hair, stomach, and wounds for as long as I can.
An impossible dream, stuck in your attention span, I feel like a fly in a spider web.

Let me in and out.
Give me the sugar-tasting love life.
This girl still plagues and still gets me in the throat.

Plays and sleep partners, the bitterness seems to mark its territory.
I don't know where she is coming or going, and I don't want to blink.
I might miss my chance to sing her to sleep every night.

I stand on this weight mixed with hope and leftover glory.
Would skip the next ten years if I knew I had her for my own. By your sound and taste, I declare myself alive.

This one is for real, for good, and hopefully
for the first time on my wavelength.

The universe will be in harmony.

Details are inclusive.
I ache from the burdens of not holding her hands. My notions are as
clear as can be, and when you see through them,
you will see me with a grin,
saying the thoughts I thought
when I first laid these eyes on her smile.

I still claim my affections; no remorse nor desire to hold back.
Just want to be her favorite toy,
locket, and any other thing that makes her smile for me.

The universe will be in harmony.

Low

It's all good.
I understand and all that jazz.

I really do miss you. I am happy that I've met you and we had
somewhat of an emotional stance together. We had a lot of fun in the
sun, in the alleys, and in the pools.

Left to my own devices,
I wouldn't explain it if I could.
Yet I fall in touch with the scandals and taste the nectar she creates with
her tongue.

The touchstone is fond memories of the softest kind.
Alas, the connection is made, and I'm restored.
In her mouth, I hide my worries, even when the burdens are too thick,
too demanding.

She is the liar, the cult, the temptation that leaves me in withdrawal.
The things that stand in our way, the muck,
the stinging, the letters never sent.

Whistle the tunes that help me get over the fact
that I have to get over you.
The courage I find is found in liquid form.
Dance the night with colorful feelings that dwell
in the warmth of the day,
while I'm soaked in the misery of your absence.

The sounds are the only release for me and the thoughts of her return.
My own mocking must be my self's attempt to let go.
Ha, I will never let go.

She Smells Like Girl, Taste Like Poison

Strings are made for control and to string the girl along.
She sulks, cuts her demons, and waits for another melting point.
Feels like a puppet, feels like a chain reaction.
Feather his ego and let him take whatever is left to care.

Insight into the madness that seeps by when you blink.
In this fear session, you start to mimic your parents' moves.
She talks to herself and whistles the tunes that comfort her through,
and sends off the energetic patterns that will break the mold.

Let her breathe.
Let her smell the roses, wine, and the boy's precious scent.
Endure this torture and save the day.
Let the love kindly break the hold and cut the strings.

Waved goodbye to the demons.
Oddly, she is finding beauty in this madness.
The boy's desires stand silently and timidly.
So quiet it doesn't quite express itself in true detail.
The lady has watched for too long and has had enough.
Let me be the only one, she screams.
Let me take away all that troubles and takes a toll.
I'll bring you more than you can find in 2,209,209,200 defeats
and triumphs.
Save the most intriguing moments for this chance.
She winks and blinks and sucks all in his honor.
These other boys can't compare, nor deliver.

Take this moment and breed it with others until we have nothing
but a zillion moments of bliss.
Taking a number till we get to go to the heavens.
We will live it, love it, and become it,
and by then, the gods will want to die and come to us.

Not as Good as the Rest

I have the biggest crush on this girl.
She smells like heaven and mimics my fondest dreams.
Want to take her apart and put her back together,
make sure every part works better, works new.

She will kiss my desires and drink my excuses away,
live with my best intentions,
and address each day with a perfect clause.

Yearn the deep,
the demand and supply of the world's burdens.
Every young boy and girl looking up for answers found only inside us,
yet the circus we oblige is constantly traveling.

You look like a miracle.
You remind me of childhood.
This is enough for the moment and will be molded into
my depths in due time.

This is no scandal, far from a joke.
My heart is pounding for this touch.
The simple explosion of your gaze and emotions will be a splendid
attempt to start smiling sincerely.
I belong in your attention span.
I devour all that is in my way of it.
Ran too much the wrong way, only to see that on the other side is you,
waiting with a beer and sounds I need to hear.

The passion I proclaim is fastened to your liking.
I do all I can to see your dancing smile.

Why don't you want the walk to be more enjoyable?
What can I do to kiss you longer?

Soundwave face, mountains stolen by rain, walk to you and see you
hiding behind snow, blowing in the blood.
4 a.m. hits you like a truck.
I awake only to see your response.
You make me want to be more, and I love it.
I love your skin, your hair, your voice, your mind, your face.
I love your all and then some.
Waltz you to the places where I demand your full attention.
This is my world.
I offer it as your pillow.
Please rest, I want you to rest from your journeys.
This one is going to be a star.
I want to be your star.
Let's burn forever together, make the sun sulk with envy.

I wish for you to answer me in good time.
Place yourself in my mind, fall in love with my view, my soul, my all.
Take the struggle away,
and if you would or could, please be gentle with me.

I will bestow the same,
and will do whatever it takes to keep you smiling till it gets stuck there,
and you fall in love with all that deserves it.

Tag Me In

Boy is threatened by demons that lurk near, shadowing his every move.
The burst that leaves me stringing along for more is sad enough to leave
all my pleasure spots behind.

This girl seeks justice, liberty, and all that follows.
She keeps this boy so well in check, creates the harmony on which this
boy bases his words, and keeps the monsters away from his castle.

He walks this world with his fingers in his eyes, poking himself rather
than looking at their ugliness.
The demands of being a conscious lad led to these addictions,
and left everything with a bad taste, even the girl's words.

Ran as much as possible till the girl was out of breath.
She sat down, drank the wine, counted his blessings, named his beauty
parts, and laid her attention intensely on his words.

The boy wants to play king of the world.
She wants to play hide and seek.
He does this in the hope that he will succeed in his tortured state,
give up on all that bugs him, and start
at the beginning of the beautiful days.
Boy meets girl, girl runs like a maniac.
Boy sulks and frowns,
drowns in self-loathing and liquids that shouldn't be mentioned...

until the moment the boy thinks of the girl's smile,
puts on his running shoes,
and makes a dash to win her heart and save the planet, at that.

Circling around me, the ugliness of feelings.
The emotional sides need just as much medicine as the rest.
Medicine is found in sounds, kisses, and childlike laughter, but mostly
in the girl who wants to play hide and seek.

Yell at me, tell me that the tunes are too loud.
You need to hear a softer, less intense view.
I can't explain to you the smell of emptiness, the smell that lingers after
you once experienced it,
but the smell of the girl is thirty zillion times more effective.

The smile she bestows is enough
to make the boy play her favorite pleasures.

About the Time I Had to Get My Own Wings

Blamed me for the misery, checked.
Setting myself up for a nasty heartache, double-checked.
You remind me of you and the stuff we used to do.
Like singing in corners and worshiping the spotlights.

Met you on a Tuesday, fell for you by Wednesday at 3:10 p.m.
Gave up on the whole eight years since I talked to you last,
without rearview mirrors, so I'd never look back.
Tattoo nostalgia for another you: legs are trembling, and wings are
convulsing with iron lungs and ironic tongues.

I called this day my own with a twist of fate, which was once a lemon.
I love you more today than ever.
I like the sound of that one; I may repeat it again.

On second thought, I will tell you something original this time:
If living in the past is the only way to have you, you will find me setting
back every clock in the world.
Instinct is intact, like growing pains and the government of Tahiti.
If you are alone, talk to your mirror-sized ego.
It will whistle the singing sensations that I hum in my coma-like sleep.

The sting, the flooding,
the cockroaches that plague the white city of hope.
I made no sense just there, like the time I didn't stay with you.

I am alone with nowhere to go.
I am here only with the sins I know.
Just a touch of greatness, just a second chance,
or 48,029,284,239 more.

I alone stand on the words of my oath: to love you more than ever.
Breathe in my direction, tingling and distant.

I wage war on your disbelief without the sands of time,
without your handling of secret displays.
Emptiness lacks its designation, with more and more collective
bargaining scenarios.
I clean myself with my self-opinions.
Take a number when you come too.
I will be waiting with all the love in my heart's residue.

There is me in the second chance of a lifetime, like bargain bidding and
counterattacking in the background.
We've gone years and years through the riptides,
and the bitterness stalking near,
with the tidal waves and the second-guessing,
the chance to catch yourself
before you realize your potential.

April showers, the girl is my favorite scenario, bells for you, and the way
you walk through my imagination.
I am sorry for you, sorry for me,
and sorry that I never stopped loving your beauty.
Kingdom come, my will is forever in love. The seething mistakes will be
replaced with left-alone, nevermore reminders, and carrying on and on
about the ministers of misconduct.

It shall never pierce our souls' skin again.
We shall carry on like the tables turning and let down feelings retrieving
to higher ground, and the sounds will be forever drowned
in the realization that we were meant to be.

Count my misery with your fingers, if you want,
but don't forget to use your toes.
Because the second I remake myself,
I will breathe in your direction and cancel out the negativity.